MUTTS
Shelter Stories
Love. Guaranteed.

Patrick
McDonnell

Foreword by **Wayne Pacelle**
President and CEO, The Humane Society of the United States

**Andrews McMeel
Publishing**®
a division of Andrews McMeel Universal

Other Books by Patrick McDonnell

Mutts
Cats and Dogs: Mutts II
More Shtuff: Mutts III
Yesh!: Mutts IV
Our Mutts: Five
A Little Look-See: Mutts VI
What Now: Mutts VII
I Want to Be the Kitty: Mutts VIII
Dog-Eared: Mutts IX
Who Let the Cat Out: Mutts X
Everyday Mutts
Animal Friendly
Call of the Wild
Stop and Smell the Roses
Earl & Mooch
Our Little Kat King
Bonk!
A Shtinky Little Christmas
Cat Crazy
Living the Dream
Playtime
Year of Yesh

Mutts Sundays
Sunday Mornings
Sunday Afternoons
Sunday Evenings

The Best of Mutts

Acknowledgments

So many people have helped with this book. I would like to thank:

My wife, Karen, for her guidance on this project and in my career.
Her smarts, creativity, and big heart have contributed immensely to my life.

Jennifer Schulz, for keeping this book on track by coordinating the entries,
working with The Humane Society of the United States to select the final photos,
and assisting in sequencing the material. Her in-depth understanding of
shelters, concern for all animals, and enthusiasm have been invaluable.

The Humane Society of the United States:
Kathy Bauch (for all she does), Adam Goldfarb, Stephanie Shain, and, of course,
The HSUS president and CEO Wayne Pacelle. Animals around the world are better off because of Wayne's
unyielding efforts and results. He has raised, and continues to raise, the bar for animal welfare.

Mutts.com:
Elena Nazzaro, Dany Petraska, Matt Wenner, Nichole Chobin, Patty Illum, Allyson Murphy.
Chintan Parikh, who set up the website coding for the Shelter Stories "Call for Entries."
And especially Rich Mansfield for providing a welcoming home for *MUTTS* on the Web.

King Features Syndicate: Glenn Mott, Claudia Smith, Frank Caruso, and Audra Kujawski.

Andrews McMeel Publishing and, in particular, my editor, Erin Friedrich, for being so cool.

Command-Z Design: Jeff Schulz, for making this book look fantastic.

Stu Rees.

And, finally, everyone who submitted photos and stories about their companion animals.
Your love, and the human-animal bond, is evident in this book and I can't thank you enough.

> "Until one has loved an animal,
> a part of one's soul remains
> unawakened." —*Anatole France*

These are some of the stories of the 10 million cats and dogs (and rabbits, ferrets, guinea pigs, birds . . .) who wind up in our animal shelters each year. They are stories about the innocent animals who patiently wait for a home, the dedicated workers who devote such care to them, and the kindhearted people who adopt them. They are stories of past cruelty, survival, sacrifice, hope, salvation—and joy.

The cartoon stories were created by me for my comic strip **MUTTS**. The others are real stories with photographs, told in the words of proud animal guardians. These are family photos—candid, honest, relaxed—taken by trusted loved ones. Just look at these companion animals. These are the lucky ones. Look into their eyes. When you take away their stories all that is left is unconditional love, staring its noble face right back at you. And that's the whole story.

Adopt some love today.

PATRICK McDONNELL

Foreword

Wayne Pacelle
President and CEO
The Humane Society of the United States

I have the lucky circumstance of calling Patrick McDonnell both a friend and professional colleague. For a decade or so, he has served on the national board of The Humane Society of the United States (HSUS), where I now serve as president. You get to know some pretty altruistic people in my line of work. And I have met few people in the animal-protection cause as capable and good-hearted as Patrick.

As one of America's most successful cartoonists, Patrick could easily have closed himself off from the problems of the world—content to draw cartoon animals without ever worrying about real ones. But he's not that kind of artist, or that kind of person. And instead he has used his gifts to bring hope and human kindness into the lives of abused and homeless animals.

Along with the laughs that his comic strip provides—in the daily doings of Earl, Mooch, Guard Dog, and the other delightful characters who inhabit **MUTTS**—Patrick's readers can always find the artist's compassionate spirit. The strips collected in *Shelter Stories* are funny, touching, and, while entertaining us, offer gentle reminders of the plight of real dogs, cats, and other animals who have no one to care for them. Unnumbered animals have been rescued and given a second chance because of **MUTTS**. And that, for Patrick McDonnell, is worth more than all his many awards and honors put together.

The problem of homeless and unwanted animals is an emotional issue for me, and not just because I am president of The HSUS. As with many others in the animal-protection movement, I can trace a path from my current job all the way back to my first encounter with an animal shelter.

Stepping out the front door of my boyhood home in New Haven, Connecticut, and looking just a little to the left, you could see the drab and forbidding figure of New Haven

(continued next page)

Animal Shelter, which at the time was run by the city police department. If you didn't know what the facility was, it would be hard to guess because it was so nondescript and impersonal. But once you linked the cacophony of barking sounds to the building, there was no mistaking that it was the pound.

As a city-run shelter, the facility was uninviting, even for a kid like me who loved animals. Few pitched in to help because it just seemed so unpleasant and depressing, and it didn't seem like the police needed help; after all, they were the ones to help the community, not the other way around. I would visit once in a while, but I did not dive in and walk the dogs or do much in the way of helping to promote adoptions. At the time, I did not know enough, and I did not make the connections. I'll always regret my lack of commitment to those dogs and cats who undoubtedly yearned for a loving gaze or a gentle pat on the head or, even better, a warm and loving new home.

But while I fault myself, I must confess that the atmospherics of these types of shelters did not encourage public engagement and participation. Whether government-run or private, so many shelters just seemed like undesirable destinations—for animals or people. They looked like prisons for animals—with bricks and fences and an austere design that made them seem like a bunker or fortress. The common name for these places—*the pound* —reinforced your instinctive reaction of a holding facility, rather than a place to meet a lifelong companion. And even today, when a politician is considered a failure or washed up, the expression is "He couldn't even run for dogcatcher," as if that's the worst job in public service. That's hardly the right branding if we want people to visit these operations and adopt an animal.

Since 1994, when Patrick created **MUTTS**, he has worked to turn around this image through the strip, which is now carried in more than 700 newspapers. He has reached millions of Americans with a different view of shelters and with a plea to connect people with animals who just want a loving home. And he has helped drive people to support local shelters. In the last decade, there has been a building explosion, with wonderful new shelters being constructed in communities throughout the nation. With works like *Shelter Stories*, Patrick is helping to transform shelters from dead-end destinations for people and animals into centers for redemption, hope, and companionship.

We Americans do have a love affair with animals, especially pets—yet we often do not know how best to help them. Buying an animal from a pet store—paying anywhere from a few hundred to a few thousand dollars—generally means you are supporting puppy mills. They are supplied with their "stock" by these commercial pet factories that churn out animals for the pet trade. Often the animals, who have never known tenderness and human affection, are poorly socialized. And because they are often inbred and poorly cared for, they are often in ill-health.

Contrast these unlucky puppy mills dogs with the animals from shelters. They are often better adjusted, because many of them lived in a home and had human companionship, or now, because they get attention from shelter workers or volunteers. And you only have to pay a modest adoption fee, not a premium price for a purebred raised in a mill. And with four to six million dogs and cats euthanized in shelters every year—many of them healthy and adoptable—there's just no good reason to obtain dogs or cats from pet stores. Loving and needy animals are right there in your community.

Pets enrich our lives in so many ways, showing us their distinctive personalities and giving us so much unconditional love. It's the finest expression of the human-animal bond. The work of Patrick McDonnell provides a pathway for any humane-minded person— turning us away from the pet trade and toward our shelters, where you can make a friend for life. This book is a credit to his life's work and passion, and I know you will enjoy it and be moved by it.

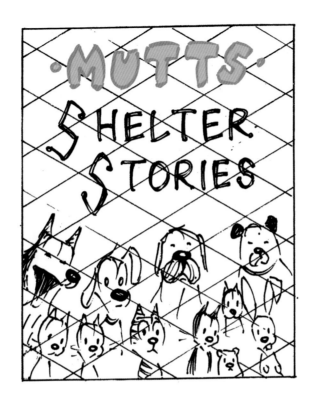

Row 1:

SHELTER STORIES  CHICKPEA AND CHICKPEA'S BROTHER

I HOPE **YOU** FIND A HOME! | I HOPE **YOU** FIND A HOME!

HEY, MAYBE YOU'LL BE PICKED **NEXT!** | **HEY,** MAYBE YOU'LL BE PICKED **NEXT!**

WE'VE BEEN CAGED TOGETHER **TOO** LONG. | WE'VE BEEN CAGED TOGETHER **TOO** LONG.

Row 2:

SHELTER STORIES  CHICKPEA AND CHICKPEA'S BROTHER

THE PERSON WHO PICKS ME IS GOING TO GET KISSED AND LICKED LIKE THERE'S **NO** TOMORROW!

THE PERSON WHO PICKS ME IS GOING TO GET PURRS AND CUDDLES **ALL** NIGHT LONG!

THE PERSON WHO PICKS ME.

SHELTER STORIES

CHICKPEA AND CHICKPEA'S BROTHER

I HOPE SOMEONE PICKS YOU TODAY!

I HOPE SOMEONE PICKS YOU TODAY!

I HOPE SOMEONE PICKS US TODAY!!!

A TWOFER!

SHELTER STORIES

CHICKPEA AND CHICKPEA'S BROTHER

HOW COME **NO**BODY EVER PICKS **ME**?

MAYBE THEY'RE LOOKING FOR SOMETHING DIFFERENT...

PICK ME.

SHELTER STORIES

CHICKPEA AND CHICKPEA'S BROTHER ©

WHAT HAPPENS IF **NO**BODY PICKS US?

NOBODY PICKS **US**!?! IMPOSSIBLE!

THE WORLD CAN'T BE **THAT** CRAZY!

SHELTER STORIES

CHICKPEA AND CHICKPEA'S BROTHER ©

WELL, THE SHELTER'S CLOSING UP FOR ANOTHER DAY...

WE DIDN'T GET PICKED.

I KNOW.

TOMORROW.

GUARANTEED.

"Oscar and Lucy were surrendered littermates. We fell in love with them instantly."

"When we first talked to **Daisy** at the shelter, her tail started wagging and she slowly wiggled toward us . . . looking sweet, hopeful, and helpless all at the same time."

"Charlotte is superintelligent, loving, loyal to a fault. She has a bag full of tricks (some useful, some not). Some say spoiled, I say 'loved to the max.'"

"My best friend."

 I KNOW WHAT IT'S LIKE TO BE ALONE IN A CAGE... WAITING FOR A KINDNESS FROM A STRANGER...

 YOU WAIT... AND WAIT... HOPING...PRAYING ...THINKING 'LIFE SHOULDN'T BE LIKE THIS'...

 YOU KNOW YOU CAN DO MORE... BE MORE... YOU HOLD ONTO THE DREAM...

 YOU JUST WISH SOMEDAY YOU COULD SHARE IT WITH SOMEONE.

 SURE ENOUGH, ONE DAY MY 'ANGEL' ANNIE CAME TO SHARE IT WITH **ME**!

 NOW, **I** HAVE A BED... A FOOD DISH... A WATER BOWL... A HOME.

 ... AND NOW IT'S **MY** TURN TO SHARE

- 13 -

"Melora was sitting in my lap at the shelter and gave me this intense, pleading look that I will never forget."

SHELTER STORIES: PERSONALS

Starting Over - SWF, highly intelligent, attractive, well-traveled, speaks French. Looking for that certain someone who still believes in love. Is it you?

SHELTER STORIES "BOWSER"

I WAS THE FIRST PICK FROM MY LITTER. MY FAMILY THOUGHT **I** WAS THE 'CUTEST LITTLE THING'. IN A YEAR... I WAS... GONE

IT WAS A MATTER OF SIZE.

I GOT BIG...

AND THEIR HEARTS GOT SMALL.

SHELTER STORIES "PIP"

I WAS A CHRISTMAS PUPPY. THE KIDS JUMPED FOR JOY THAT MORNING. IT WAS VERY EXCITING.

BUT NOT AS EXCITING AS THEIR NEW VIDEO GAMES..... MY DAYS WERE NUMBERED.

NOW I'M WAITING FOR **MY** SANTA TO COME.

"Scatter was surrendered to the shelter because she was getting too big. She is sweet, obedient, smart, and is the perfect size for us!"

I'm a "keeper"!

SHELTER STORIES "Tom-Tom"

YOU'RE **RIGHT**, BUSHY! THIS HOUSE **DOES** NEED A **PET**!

I'M GOING TO CALL OUR **LOCAL** ANIMAL SHELTER RIGHT **NOW**!

MAY **I** TALK TO ONE OF THE KITTIES?

SHELTER STORIES "Tom-Tom"

THIS IS MY **BIG** CHANCE FOR ADOPTION. I'VE CLEANED MYSELF UP. NOW I JUST HAVE TO LOOK CUTE AND

THINK POSITIVE!

I'M A "KEEPER." I'M A "KEEPER." **I'M A "KEEPER."**

"Wammes has the most beautiful big eyes.

I fell in love with him the moment I saw him."

SHELTER STORIES

"PETUNIA"

WHAT'S THIS—
A BEAUTY CONTEST
!?!

SO I'M NOT THE CUTEST DOGGY HERE...

...I'D EASILY WIN MISS CONGENIALITY.

"Elvis: His mug says it all."

"This is the day that **Willie** came home with me."

SHELTER STORIES ①

"JAZ"

IT'S EASY. YOU LOCATE YOUR NEAREST SHELTER.

YOU GO DOWN THERE AND YOU PICK OUT THE CUTEST KITTY!

ME.

"Once neglected and underfed, Luna now enjoys home-cooked meals."

HANDLE WITH CARE
THIS SIDE UP

"Jaz and Jules were two of 53 cats
rescued from an overcrowded house.
They are sweet, loving, and purr purr machines."

SHELTER STORIES
"EENIE MINNIE MYNEE AND MOE"

MY SISTERS AND I WERE SAVED FROM AN ABANDONED BUILDING.
... COLD...
... WET...
.. SCARED...

NOW WE'RE JUST WAITING FOR A HOME.

ANY HOME.

ONE WITH A ROOF WOULD BE NICE.

SHELTER STORIES
"TOM·TOM"

I LIVED MY WHOLE LIFE ON THE STREETS —UNTIL I WAS RESCUED AND BROUGHT HERE.

MANY PEOPLE COME AND LOOK AT ME—BUT NO TAKERS...
... SO FAR.

I DON'T KNOW WHAT THEY'RE **SO** WORRIED ABOUT...

I'M NOT TOO PICKY.

"Folks will know how large your
soul is by the way you treat
a dog." —*Charles F. Duran*

"This is **Fannie**'s idea of a good time."

"Social butterfly."

Sake and Sushi

"We couldn't adopt Chickpea

without his brother!"

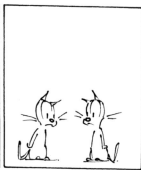

SHELTER STORIES

CHICKPEA AND CHICKPEA'S BROTHER

CHICKPEA FINALLY GOT ADOPTED! *YAHOO!*

HOW EXCITING! I CAN'T WAIT TO TELL...

...CHICKPEA...

SHELTER STORIES

CHICKPEA AND CHICKPEA'S BROTHER

CHICKPEA FINALLY GOT **ADOPTED!**

IT'S A DREAM COME TRUE. I COULDN'T BE HAPPIER!

SHNIFF

"Born on the streets, Squirt and Fuzzy became 'roommates' while awaiting adoption. They're best friends."

"If the only prayer you say in life is thank you, that would suffice." —*Meister Eckhart*

"Inseparable."

"**Castor** and **Pollux** were left behind in an
empty apartment. We felt the two had been through so much,
it was time they came home . . . together."

"Max was nervous and scared, but I could see the heart this dog had, and I knew that with some love and attention, he would flourish."

"Has learned over 20 tricks."

Row 1:

SHELTER STORIES — ANDY

ME.

YOU?

ME AND YOU!

Row 2:

SHELTER STORIES — ANDY

THIS IS THE ROOM WE TEST EACH OTHER OUT IN.

LICK LICK LICK

SHE TASTES GOOD TO ME!

SHELTER STORIES

ANDY

I THINK SHE'S FILLING OUT THE ADOPTION PAPERS.

THAT'S ANDY WITH A "Y".

SHELTER STORIES

ANDY

I'M GOING **OUT!** I'M GOING **HOME!**

SHNIFF

IS IT ME OR IS IT GETTING MISTY OUT HERE?

Strip 1:

 SHELTER STORIES ANDY

I'M AFRAID TO OPEN MY EYES. I'M AFRAID YESTERDAY WAS **ALL** A DREAM AND I'LL WAKE UP AND STILL BE IN THE SHELTER

 'SIGH'... **OKAY**, I'VE GOT TO OPEN THEM. HERE GOES... ONE... TWO... **THREE**!

Strip 2:

 SHELTER STORIES ANDY

MY NEW HOME

MY NEW FOOD BOWL

MY NEW BED

MY HERO!

"Zoë was found running

with a pack of stray dogs

outside of JFK airport.

I volunteered to foster her,

but I knew at first sight that

she was my forever dog.

After 9/11,
Zoë was
honored
for her
therapy
work."

"Misty was found by the side of a busy road.
The image of this terrified kitty clinging to the curb,
too scared to move, touched me. Today she specializes
in unexpected displays of affection."

SHELTER STORIES: PERSONALS

Lonely? Me too - Recent orphan wants to love again. Seeks soul mate for a new beginning. You will not believe your luck.

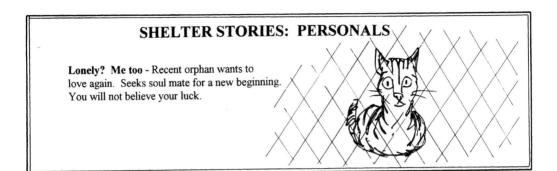

SHELTER STORIES

EMMA

IT WAS GETTING VERY LONELY TRYING TO LIVE BY MYSELF... UNTIL SOMEONE SAID I SHOULD ADOPT A MATURE PET FROM THE SHELTER.

NOW, I HAVE A LOVELY NEW MAN AROUND THE HOUSE!

...AND THIS ONE DOESN'T SNORE...

SHELTER STORIES: PERSONALS

Sweet Brown Eyes - I am nine years young - petite, fetching, radiant, yet down to earth. Looking for a committed relationship. No psychos or phonies, please.

SHELTER
o
STORIES

ELIZABETH

WHEN I WENT TO MY LOCAL SHELTER THERE WAS THIS BIG, FURRY, WHITE DOG WITH A FUNNY BARK THAT **NO** ONE WANTED!

BOY, WAS **I** LUCKY.

WOMF!

"Surrendered at seven years of age, Ollie's big brown eyes and gentle kisses melted my heart."

Shelter Stories
"SHEMP"

I'M THE "OLDER" DOG IN THE SHELTER

SURE... MAYBE I DON'T **RUN** AS FAST OR **JUMP** AS HIGH... ...BUT...

I CAN STILL **LICK** A FACE WITH THE BEST OF 'EM!

Shelter Stories
"SHEMP"

THIS IS NATIONAL ANIMAL SHELTER APPRECIATION WEEK.

WHY NOT GO VISIT YOUR LOCAL SHELTER AND TAKE A LOOK AT US "OLDER" DOGS

WE'D **REALLY** APPRECIATE IT!

SHELTER STORIES ⊙ "SHEMP"

I'M NOT "OLD"...

I'M "MATURE"... "WELL-SEASONED"... "EXPERIENCED"...

..."AVAILABLE."

SHELTER STORIES ⊙ "SHEMP"

AN OLDER DOG MAKES FOR A **GREAT** COMPANION

WE'RE **VERY** LOVING AND EASYGOING.

... JUST DON'T CALL ME "POPS."

I DON'T WANNA BE OLD!!!

"Ten-year-old **Tammy** likes to sleep in

the sun during the day . . .

and on my bed at night."

SHELTER
STORIES ©
"SHEMP"

WHO SAYS YOU CAN'T TEACH AN **OLD** DOG **NEW** TRICKS?

MAYBE **YOU**'LL GO TO YOUR SHELTER AND GET A MATURE DOG WHO'LL MAKE YOUR **BLUES** DISAPPEAR !!!

HOW'S **THAT** FOR TRICKS!

SHELTER
STORIES ©
"SHEMP"

I GOT PICKED! **WOW!** **NO** MORE CAGES !!!

MAYBE I'LL SEE YOU OUT THERE IN THE "FREE" **WORLD**...

I'LL BE THE GUY ROLLING IN THE CLOVER.

"Despite being returned by

three different families,

nine-year-old Zoe's spunk

and determination

captured our hearts."

Thunder:

adopted at age nine

"When he finally realized
that this was his forever home,
he settled into his new bed.
Did I mention that he snores
louder than my husband?"

"Lucky."

"Intelligent."

Petunia:

adopted at age 10

"We saw a diamond
in the rough and knew
she was meant for us."

Zara:

adopted at age 11

"We knew that she still had lots of love to give."

"Beautiful."

"Expressive."

Nini:

adopted at age seven

"When Nini arrived at the shelter, she had a growth on her nose, part of her ear was missing, and she was underweight. When we met, she leapt onto my shoulder and started purring. We are blessed that we found her."

UNWANTED

UNTHINKABLE

UNAVOIDABLE

ANIMAL CONTRO

UNCHOSEN
(UNBEARABLE)

UNCAGED...

UNBELIEVABLE!!!

PURRRR

"Bindi's story and little face melted my heart. Formally fearful of closed spaces, she now sleeps under the covers with me."

Row 1:

SHELTER STORIES ◦ OLIVE

I WAS RAISED ON THE CITY STREETS. THAT MAKES ME A "FERAL" CAT.

FERAL MEANS WILD.

BELIEVE ME— I WASN'T TOO WILD ABOUT IT.

Row 2:

SHELTER STORIES ◦ OLIVE

LIVING ON THE STREETS, MY MOM FED US TO START, BUT SOON WE HAD TO LEARN TO FEND FOR OUR-SELVES.

I'LL BE ETERNALLY GRATEFUL TO MY DEAR MOTHER

...AND **ALL** OF THE LITTER BUGS.

 **SHELTER STORIES** OLIVE

YESTERDAY I WAS OUT ON THE COLD STREETS.

TODAY I'M IN A WARM SHELTER.

I HAVE HIGH HOPES FOR TOMORROW.

 **SHELTER STORIES** OLIVE

I WAS A "FERAL KITTY."

NOW I'M A "SHELTER KITTY."

WHAT COULD BE NEXT...?

"YOUR" KITTY!

"What greater gift than the love of a cat?"
—*Charles Dickens*

"Yoda was born a feral kitten and was not expected to survive. Once her fur grew in, she never looked back."

"Gentle."

"Beloved."

"Isabella was a feral barn cat. I met her while volunteering. I visited her every day until she could be handled, then brought her home.

"Candy was captured on a Navy base. Now she loves to be with the family and follows me around the house."

"Sweet and calm."

"A beauty."

"Pickles was being overlooked because of her color, age, and shyness. She needed a loving home and time to come out of her shell. That home was ours."

"Rena was the feistiest spitfire I'd ever seen, but we bonded.

From the street life to the good life."

"Enchanting."

"Casper

was the kindest,

most generous little

dog I had ever

encountered."

"Born on the mean streets of Brooklyn, **Banjo**'s life is now filled with love, stability, and lots of green grass. Nothing makes him happier than playing with his toys or snuggling with his kitty friends."

"Charlie wanted to be
doted on from the beginning.
He had the cutest butterball belly.
He's our dog of a lifetime."

SHELTER STORIES: PERSONALS

Me: Warmhearted, spirited, fun, affectionate, waiting.
You: Kind, genuine, tender, compassionate,
come and get me.

 SHELTER STORIES DAVE

 MUTTS ARE THE BEST DOGS AROUND.

 MY MAX IS A LITTLE PART SHEPHERD, A LITTLE PART COLLIE, AND A **BIG** PART

 ...OF MY LIFE.

"Intelligent."

"Patches was born to a rescued stray in a foster home. She is now on her way to becoming a great therapy dog."

SHELTER STORIES

"PETER"

THE KIDS WERE SO HAPPY TO GET ME THAT SUNDAY MORNING. BUT...

SOON I WAS FORGOTTEN IN A CAGE IN THE BACKYARD— AND THEN I WAS TOSSED OUT ONTO A SMALL DIRT FIELD.

THE CHOCOLATE BUNNY LASTED LONGER.

"Renfield
is a real
cuddle-
bunny."

"Popcorn was surrendered for unknown reasons. He is cuddly, entertaining, and gives kisses."

SHELTER STORIES

WHEN YOU GO TO YOUR LOCAL ANIMAL SHELTER—I SAY— START SMALL— GET A HAMSTER!	WE'RE VERY EASY TO LIVE WITH— **NO** TROUBLE AT ALL!		OKAY. SOMETIMES I HOG THE WHEEL.

SHELTER STORIES

SOME PEOPLE THINK THERE ARE **NO** PURE BREEDS AT THEIR LOCAL ANIMAL SHELTER.	WELL, TAKE A LOOK AROUND—I SEE COLLIES AND SCOTTIES AND ENGLISH SPANIELS AND...	ME.	ONE HUNDRED PERCENT HAMSTER.

"We were ready to
welcome another unwanted
guinea pig into our lives,
and there she was.

Sweet Pea

is extremely gentle and
so patient. She stands
on her back legs

doing
the cute."

"Oy is so enthusiastic

about everything.

I love the joy he

finds in life."

SHELTER STORIES

"FLOP"

OKAY—
EVERYBODY'S
GOING TO
THE SHELTER
THINKING—
"DOG"-"CAT."

I SAY:
"THINK
BUNNY."

BUNNY...
BUNNY...
BUNNY...

GOOD
THINKING.

"Bunz O'Hare

was formerly a classroom pet.

When I adopted him, he was litterbox trained,

so he did learn something at school!"

"Loving."

"**Dander** is congenitally blind and could not assimilate with the other birds. I'm an optometrist and have a special affinity for him."

"Lily was found in a shopping center parking lot with a badly broken leg. Now she likes to race people up the stairs, and when she jumps, she flies. 'Handicapped' is not in her vocabulary!"

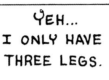

Strip 1:

| SHELTER STORIES "EDDIE·DO" | SOMEHOW I WAS ABLE TO RIP MY LEG OUT OF THAT TRAPPER'S STEEL-JAWED LEGHOLD TRAP. | BUT AS FAR AS **I** KNOW... | HIS HEART AND MIND ARE STILL TRAPPED IN IT. |

Strip 2:

| SHELTER STORIES "EDDIE·DO" | CAUGHT IN A STEEL-JAWED TRAP, I LOST MY LEG... | ... **AND** MY TRUST IN HUMANS... (I THOUGHT) | BUT I FOUND THAT AGAIN AT THE SHELTER. |

SHELTER **S**TORIES

"EDDIE·DO"

FOUR LEGS...
THREE LEGS...
No LEGS...

I'M STILL JUST
"EDDIE·DO"

ALL ME.

SHELTER **S**TORIES

"EDDIE·DO"

YUP...I LEARNED
TO GET AROUND
ON THREE LEGS.

No
BIG
DEAL.

I WONDER HOW
YOU MANAGE
ON JUST TWO.

"Little Hollers

had been to adoption day

three times without anyone

paying attention to her. I felt

she deserved a good home with

tons of love. We love her more

than anything and are so

glad we found her . . .

she is
truly
beautiful
to us."

"Incredibly kind."

"Skye has the most earnest face I had ever seen. Deaf animals have lots to offer, they just don't get the opportunity to offer it. Skye listens as well as any of my hearing dogs did, and I'm so glad I listened to my heart and brought her home."

SHELTER STORY NEWS

Beau: Found wandering the streets. Help him find a home.

Peanut: Lost and forgotten, a tiny kitten with a big heart.

Chickpea and her brother: Surrendered littermates.

Uma: Dropped off. Give her a second chance.

Rosie: Abandoned, rescued and waiting.

Stanley: Lived under a truck. Loves everybody.

"It was meant to be. Zoey needed me and I needed her."

"When we met **Lexus** on adoption day,

her overall
sweetness sealed
the deal."

"Her big baby blue eyes

took my breath away.

Finnegan jumped into

the carrier . . . I knew she wanted

to come home with me."

"Everything is better
after a good belly rub."

"Maggie Mae would not

stop springing up and down

until I came over to her.

In all honesty,

she picked me."

Every animal

dreams

of a good home.

"Reva was a stray cat who gave birth in the shelter. After all of her kittens were adopted, she spent over a year waiting to be discovered. When we read her story and saw her beautiful eyes, we couldn't leave her in that cage another minute."

"Goofy."

"Pauline

thinks that

everything is

a toy for her."

SHELTER
STORIES

"TESS"

YES! YES!
IT HAS BEEN FUN.

IT WAS NICE
MEETING YOU, TOO.

HOW ABOUT NEXT
TIME WE GO TO
YOUR PLACE...?

SHELTER
STORIES

"TESS"

...WELL... YOU
THINK ABOUT IT...

...SURE...SURE...
...I UNDERSTAND...
...**NO** PRESSURE...

YOU KNOW WHERE
TO FIND ME.

ADOPT
A
DOG
TODAY

"General Patton was hiding in the back of the cage with his head down. He had been used as a 'bait dog' for dog fights, so he gets frightened easily, but always finds the courage to be brave. He's warm, zippy, and loves his treats!"

"Diamond's face was so expressive

and his personality was so joyous, we

knew adoption was the only option.

We were hooked. He lives in a world

of love with his feline friends."

"We couldn't break them up,
so we adopted them both."

"Bonnie and Clyde roamed the streets together.
They are always very good . . . even when they are being bad."

"Oliver and Olivia
were found at a construction
site covered by debris.
We saw them in the paper and
knew they were meant for us.
They would help make our
new house into a real home."

"We are so thankful for Skippy and want to erase all of the hardship he had prior to becoming part of our family."

"I chose **Pirate** because I thought he had no chance to be chosen.

It's been 17 years now, and we have a special connection . . .

like symbiosis. Rooms are empty without Pirate."

THOSE TWO WERE MADE FOR EACH OTHER.

"Madison has the sweetest brown eyes and an Elvis Presley smile that melts your heart. He is a 'Velcro' dog as he always stays close to me. He is my protector and my love."

Mutts

Shelter Stories

"FLASH"

I'm a greyhound, a racing greyhound.

I spent the first three years of my life either in a cage or out racing. Racing, racing, racing.

I always lost.

I was determined 'useless' and was to be 'weeded out.'

Then a greyhound rescue group saved me and found me a loving home and family.

I raced to their open arms.

I finally won.

"Statuesque."

"Chai ran 141 races in her career.
She wasn't a companion animal,
but I knew I could show her what
the good life was all about.
We adore Chai and happily,
wonderfully, it is mutual."

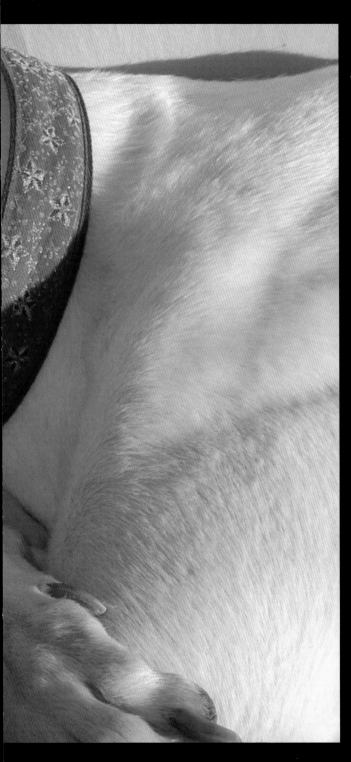

"Sharlotte, formerly known as 'Stonesider,'

was a racing greyhound.
I always wanted a dog that
would curl up in my lap and
sleep at the foot of my bed.
I had imagined that
would be a little dog.
However, that describes
Sharlotte perfectly."

"Moko Chan was trying her best
to be charming and friendly, but no one seemed to
notice her except me. After three weeks, I asked my husband
to come with me to see this sweetie and she came home
with us that evening. She carries her toys from room
to room following her bliss."

"Silly, sweet, and adorable."

"Riley, a retired therapy dog who is blind in one eye, was quite popular with the children at the local hospital. He now spends his golden years taking long walks and meeting new kitty friends."

"Sadie adopted me.

She climbed into my lap,

all 90 pounds of her,

and very calmly exhaled

with a giant sigh of relief."

 **S**HELTER **S**TORIES "SAMMY"

OKAY—SO MY FIRST OWNERS DIDN'T APPRECIATE ME ...SIGH...

IT'S THEIR LOSS.

AND YOUR GAIN?

 **S**HELTER **S**TORIES "BRANDO"

I'M NEW AROUND HERE.

DO YOU KNOW WHERE I CAN FIND A GOOD LAP IN THIS TOWN?

"Tilly was found tied to a tree.
We met and she was just what I was
looking for . . . happy, loving, sensitive."

"Timber was chained behind an abandoned building . . .
emaciated, petrified, and covered with burn scars. I knew his adoption
chances were slim because he was older and physically and
psychologically affected. After a lot of love and patience, he has become
a wonderful companion. He LOVES running in our backyard!"

"Angel has brought our family closer together.

She has taught us the true meaning of love and happiness."

"Abbie was rescued from the wreckage of the Gulf Port shelter in the wake of Hurricane Katrina. Her rescuers believe that she may have been forced to swim in her cage for six hours to keep from drowning. Her favorite thing is playing in the snow, something she would never have been able to do had she lived her life in Mississippi. The only thing she doesn't like is rain, and who could blame her for that?"

"Lovable."

"After surviving
Hurricane Katrina,
Ernie and **Bert**
live a luxurious 'California life'
filled with morning wrestling
matches and six-hour snoozes."

"Playful."

"**Guffy** was found in one
of the worst-flooded areas
of New Orleans. We thought
he deserved a loving family
to care for him after what
he had been through."

"Gregarious."

"Abandoned after Hurricane
Charlie, **Rusty** gives
unconditional love to all
the children he meets
as a therapy dog."

"**Maddie,** a refugee
from Hurricane Katrina,
loves to pull books out of
the shelves. We are sure
she reads at night."

"Devoted."

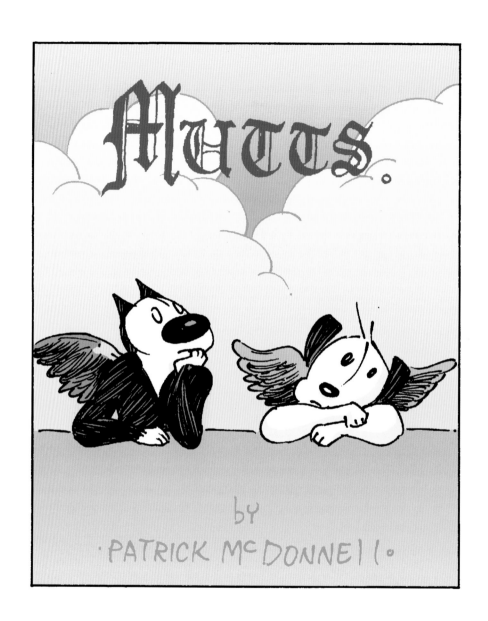

ONE FED ME...   ONE WASHED ME...   ONE FIXED UP MY BUSTED LEG...

THEY ALL HELD ME...   SO I WOULDN'T FEEL SO ALONE IN THIS BIG OL' WORLD...

| SHELTER STORIES ○ "GRETCHEN" | THERE'S GRETCHEN. SHE'S BEEN CARING FOR ANIMALS FOR A LONG TIME. | IF SHE COULD — SHE WOULD TAKE US **ALL** HOME. | IF ONLY HER HOUSE WAS AS **BIG** AS HER HEART. |

| SHELTER STORIES ○ "MARJORIE" | THAT'S MARJORIE! SHE LOGS IN MANY LONG HOURS AT THE SHELTER — BUT SHE ALWAYS HAS A SMILE. | SHE'S A **GOOD** ONE. | I'D ADOPT **HER**. |

"Allen came to the shelter as a stray just days before Christmas.

I adopted him to ensure his last days were spent in peace and comfort.

I was blessed by his affection during those few days."

"A happy girl."

"Seven-year-old Hailee was rescued from a backyard, chained up without food or water. As a volunteer at her shelter, I took her to adoption events every weekend, and nobody even looked at her. So I adopted her!"

SHELTER STORIES ○ "DR. WOO"

HERE'S DR. WOO, THE VET. SHE VOLUNTEERS AT THE SHELTER.

SHE SAYS "IT IS IN GIVING THAT WE RECEIVE."

... AND THAT'S THE BEST MEDICINE.

SHELTER STORIES ○ "RACHEL"

AHH, RACHEL. SHE'S DEDICATED HER **WHOLE** LIFE TO HELP US. ... SO, SO MANY OF US.

SOMETIMES... I SEE HER CRY.

I WISH I COULD HELP **HER**.

SHELTER
STORIES
◦
"PAUL"

THERE'S
OFFICER PAUL!
HE RESCUES
ANIMALS...

THE INJURED...
THE ABUSED...
THE LOST...
THE ABANDONED...

WE
SALUTE YOU,
OFFICER PAUL.

SHELTER
STORIES
◦
"TIDBIT"

THE VOLUNTEERS
HERE HAVE TAUGHT
ME **SO** MUCH ABOUT
DEVOTION, DEDICATION,
COMPASSION AND LOVE.

SIGH...

NOW, I JUST
NEED A **HOME**
TO SHOW'EM WHAT
I LEARNED.

"Affectionate, inquisitive, adorable, and ready for his close-up . . . Lance. It is a privilege to be his guardian."

$\mathcal{S}$HELTER $\mathcal{S}$TORIES ⊙

"TUGS"

WHAT ARE YOU WAITING FOR!?!

YOU! ME!

IT'S A NO-BRAINER.

"This is happy Yoshi enjoying his new life."

Adoption Guide

1. Where to Adopt Your Pet

- **Animal shelters** are a great place to adopt an animal. They have adult dogs and cats as well as puppies and kittens available for adoption. There's usually a wide assortment of purebred and mixed-breed animals, and many shelters adopt out other animals, too, like rabbits, guinea pigs, hamsters, birds, and fish.

- **Rescue groups** are like animal shelters, but usually they don't have a building out of which they operate; instead, they often use a network of foster homes. Rescue groups vary greatly. While some rescue groups adopt out only specific breeds of dogs or cats, others work with specific animals, like rabbits, and still others adopt out many different types of animals. If you'd like to find the rescue groups in your community, your local animal shelter may be able to help.

- **Adoption-friendly pet stores** such as Petco and PetSmart (and some other adoption-friendly pet stores) offer dogs and cats for adoption through their local animal shelters and rescue groups.

- **The Internet** can be a great place to start your search for that special new friend. Many animal shelters and rescue groups have websites where you can view their adoptable animals. Also, specialty websites, such as **PetFinder** (**www.PetFinder.com**) and **Adopt-a-Pet.com** (**www.adoptapet.com**), allow you to search for certain animals or breeds, or to do a broader search of available animals in your community.

2. How to Choose the Right Pet

- Once you've made the decision to adopt a new member into your family, how do you decide which animal will be the best fit? Should your new friend be young or old? Big or small? Fur, fins, or feathers? These are all important questions. When choosing a new animal, the best thing that you can do is take an honest look at yourself and your family. Think about your daily routines and how much time you have for a pet. And don't forget to think about your finances and living arrangement. Even though it's tempting to take home the first adorable puppy you see, that dog might not be a good match. Your family could be better suited to an older dog, or a cat, or even a mouse. It's essential to do research about different animals and different breeds so you can select a companion who truly fits your life.

(*continued next page*)

3. What to Expect from the Adoption Process

- Shelters and rescue groups ask a lot of questions of prospective adopters for two reasons: to be sure those prospective adopters are able to meet the needs of their new pets and to help ensure a good match. Even though an adopting family may have the best intentions, many animals lose their homes because families aren't prepared to properly care for a new pet or they simply choose an animal who isn't a good match. While some questions might seem intrusive, try to remember they are asked to ensure that an adopted animal is going to a home for life. Since many shelters and rescue groups have information about their adoption process on their websites, you can know in advance what to expect. Examining the adoption process thoroughly beforehand can save time and prevent confusion.

4. Post-Adoption Resources

- Behavior problems can be an issue for new pet owners. While there's no greater feeling than bringing a new pet home, it only takes a stained carpet or scratched couch to sour feelings about a new friend. Don't despair though; sometimes you just need to allow your new family member some time to adjust. There are countless resources available to help manage these problems if they continue. In many cases, the shelter or rescue group from which you adopted your new friend may be able to help. Also, there is a wide range of resources online or in your local bookstores and libraries.
- If you'd like to find a local trainer, The Humane Society of the United States offers tips on its website (**HumaneSociety.org** search **"trainer"**).
- For free pet behavior tips visit **HumaneSociety.org/PetsForLife**.
- Veterinary care is important for all companion animals. When choosing a veterinarian, don't rely solely on location. Just because an animal hospital is close to home, doesn't mean it's the right one for you. To learn how to select a veterinarian, visit **HumaneSociety.org** and search **"veterinarian."**